T0156615

God Is Great

A Collection *of* Poems

Marcia Grace Stewart Goulbourne

BALBOA.PRESS
A DIVISION OF HAY HOUSE

Balboa Press books may be ordered through booksellers or by contacting:

Balboa Press
A Division of Hay House
1663 Liberty Drive
Bloomington, IN 47403
www.balboapress.com
844-682-1282

Because of the dynamic nature of the Internet, any web addresses or
links contained in this book may have changed since publication and
may no longer be valid. The views expressed in this work are solely those
of the author and do not necessarily reflect the views of the publisher,
and the publisher hereby disclaims any responsibility for them.

The author of this book does not dispense medical advice or prescribe
the use of any technique as a form of treatment for physical, emotional,
or medical problems without the advice of a physician, either directly
or indirectly. The intent of the author is only to offer information
of a general nature to help you in your quest for emotional and
spiritual well-being. In the event you use any of the information in
this book for yourself, which is your constitutional right, the author
and the publisher assume no responsibility for your actions.

Any people depicted in stock imagery provided by Getty Images are
models, and such images are being used for illustrative purposes only.
Certain stock imagery © Getty Images.

Print information available on the last page.

ISBN: 978-1-9822-5218-2 (sc)
ISBN: 978-1-9822-5219-9 (e)

Balboa Press rev. date: 01/06/2021

PRODUCED BY:

Home of MIXED BREED

📞 or text (305) 338-6512
✉ dgoul001@fiu.edu
🌐 miamibreedrecords.com

🙂 mixedbreed Ego Trip n' Fall
ⓕ mixedbreedtheband
🅾 mixedbreedtheband
🅾 mixedbreed
🅿 mixedbreed
🅾 mixedbreed
🅾 mixedbreed
🅾 mixedbreed
🅾 mixedbreed
🅾 mixedbreedmusic@hotmail.com

Donald Goulbourne
President

Rock/Garage/Metal

Contents

A BLESSED SONG

God Is Great

DATE: JUNE 20th 2004

VERSE (1)

GOD IS GREAT, THE ONE WE ALL SHOULD
TRUST.
BE ASSURED, HE IS NOT UNJUST.
BEYOND ANY DOUBT OR FEAR,
TALK TO HIM, HE IS CERTAIN TO HEAR.
HE IS ALWAYS BY OUR SIDE,
FROM DAWN TO DARK, HE WILL BE OUR
GUIDE.

VERSE (2)

GOD IS GREAT, HE IS THE PLANNER WHO HAS ASSIGNMENTS FOR EVERY FLAG AND BANNER
THE ALMIGHTY STRONG AND POWERFUL, KEEP HIS WORLD RIGHTEOUS AND PEACEFUL
CHERISH EVERY MOMENT, EACH DAY WE AWAKE,
DO IT PLEASE, FOR HIS GOODNESS SAKE.

VERSE (3)

GOD IS GREATER THAN THE LIGHTENING
AND THE THUNDER.
SO BE AT YOUR BEST, DO NOT BLUNDER.
HE KNOWS EVERY THOUGHT, SEES EVERY
MOTION,
AND WILL REWARD ACCORDING TO OUR
ACTION.
GREATER NOW AND ALWAYS
LET US BE THANKFUL FOR ALL OUR DAYS.

VERSE (4)

GOD IS GREAT, THE VERY BEST FRIEND,
INITIALLY AND TO THE END.
BE CONFIDENT, HAVE NO FEAR,
FOR HE IS EVER LOVING, EVER NEAR.
AFFIRMATIVE AND POSITIVE,
HE IS FOREVER EFFECTIVE.

A BLESSED SONG

A Nice Day

DATE: MAY 24ᵀᴴ, 2004

VERSE (1)

THE RISING SUN BRINGS THE MORNING BLISS,
A CHIRP FROM THE BIRDS I COULD NOT MISS;
FLYING AROUND SO HAPPY AND FREE,
RESTING ON EVERY LIMB OF TREE.
THEN FLAPPING THEIR WINGS AROUND AND ABOVE,
FINALLY MAKING IT TO THE HOME OF THE DOVE.

CHORUS:

OH! WHAT A NICE DAY;
LET US ENJOY
THE BEAUTY I SAY;
COME WHAT MAY.

VERSE (2)

LET KINDNESS AND HONESTY BE THE
TREAT,
WITH EVERYONE WE MAY MEET.
THE GREEN GRASS AND EARTH,
SUPPORT OUR FEET
WITH EVERY STEP OF MIRTH.
LET NATURE CONTINUE IT'S SPECIAL CARE,
TO ALL THAT IS BRIGHT AND FAIR.

CHORUS:

OH! WHAT A NICE DAY;
LET US ENJOY
THE BEAUTY I SAY;
COME WHAT MAY.

VERSE (3)

THE FLOWERS SURELY BRING US CHEER,
FOR FAMILY AND FRIENDS FAR AND NEAR.
TWILIGHT GLIDES THE SKIES,
WHEN ALL THE EXCITEMENT OF THE DAY
DIES.
THEN THE SUNSET TAKES ITS PLACE
TO COMPLETE THE DAY WITH GRACE.

CHORUS:

OH! WHAT A NICE DAY;
LET US ENJOY
THE BEAUTY I SAY;
COME WHAT MAY.

VERSE (4)

THE COLOR OF DARKNESS THEN APPEARS,
MAKING US SLEEPY TO AVOID OUR FEARS
THE TWINKLING OF THE STARS; THE LIGHT
OF THE MOON
REMIND US THERE IS ANOTHER BLESSED
DAY COMING SOON.

CHORUS:

OH! WHAT A NICE DAY;
LET US ENJOY
THE BEAUTY I SAY;
COME WHAT MAY.

A BLESSED SONG

"You"

DATE: JUNE 5th, 2004

VERSE (1)

BELIEVE IN YOU RIGHT FROM THE START,
GOOD INTENTIONS ARE IN YOUR HEART,
YOU ARE CREATED TO BE TRUE,
THERE IS NO DOUBT WHAT IS MEANT
FOR YOU.

CHORUS:

SO WHY WONDER WHAT OR WHO?
LET'S JUST THINK ABOUT YOU.

VERSE (2)

ALWAYS ADVANCE, DON'T LOOK BEHIND,
SPILT MILK YOU WILL NEVER FIND.
CLIMB OVER ALL THE HURDLES, NEAR
AND FAR,
NO PONDERING, YOU ARE BORN TO BE A
STAR.

CHORUS:

SO WHY WONDER WHAT OR WHO?
LET'S JUST THINK ABOUT YOU.

VERSE (3)

RISE HIGH ABOVE ALL THE PUT DOWN,
WHETHER YOU ARE FROM THE COUNTRY
OR THE TOWN.
FORGETTING HOW HARD THE STRUGGLE
MAY SEEM,
REMEMBER, YOU ARE YOUR BEST TEAM.

CHORUS:

SO WHY WONDER WHAT OR WHO?
LET'S JUST THINK ABOUT YOU.

VERSE(4)

YOU ARE BLESSED THEREFORE YOU WILL
PROGRESS,
CROWNING YOUR EFFORTS WITH SUCCESS.
KEEP YOUR ESTEEM HIGH AND CLEVER,
YOU ARE IMPORTANT TODAY AND FOREVER.

CHORUS:

SO WHY WONDER WHAT OR WHO?
LET'S JUST THINK ABOUT YOU.

A BLESSED SONG

The Minority's Creed

DATE: NOV. 29th 2004

VERSE (1)

DON'T GIVE UP THE DREAM,
IT'S REAL LIKE PEACHES AND CREAM.
NATIONALITIES AND RACES HAVE
COMBINED,
FLICKERING WITH YOUR THOUGHTS AND
MIND,
LIKE THE FLAG, RED, WHITE AND BLUE,
IT'S HARD TO REVEAL THE TRUE YOU.
THE NEW GENERATION IS A GRAND MIXED
BREED,
WHICH REVEALS THE ETHNICITY OF THIS
CREED.

VERSE (2)

SOME NEIGHBORHOODS HAVE NO
SIDEWALKS FOR YOU TO STROLL.
THERE'S SO MUCH NEED, YOU FEEL TO
SHOUT AND ROLL.
YOU ARE ALSO AFRAID TO FIND A BASE,
FOR YOU DO NOT WANT TO END UP AS A
CASE.
THE STREET LIGHTS ARE SO FAR APART,
IF YOU DRIVE AT NIGHTS, YOU ARE SCARED
TO PARK,
THE PLACE IS DIFFERENT INDEED.
BUT THAT IS THE MINORITY'S CREED.

VERSE (3)

PRIVILEGES AND REWARDS ARE FOR ALL
WHO STRIVE AT PLAYING THE BALL.
THE GAME HAS MADE MANY MILLIONAIRES,
WHO SETS THE PACE FOR OTHERS WHO
CARES.
THE MUSIC INDUSTRY HAS OPEN THE DOOR
FOR MANY MINORITIES WHO KNOW THERE
HAD TO BE MORE.
IT IS THE OUTCOME AND RESULTS WE READ
THAT MAKES US WONDER ABOUT THIS
CREED

VERSE (4)

THE COLLEGE IS THE PLACE TO BE.
TO SAY THE PLEDGE FOR YOU AND ME.
THIS EDUCATION WILL GIVE THE PUSH
TO THOSE WHO REFUSE TO KEEP SILENT
AND HUSH.
SO BACK TO SCHOOL AND READ THE BOOK,
UNLESS YOU PREFER TO STAND AND COOK.
GET THE DEGREE TO HELP YOU SUCCEED
AND SHINE LIKE A STAR FOR THE MINORITY'S
CREED.

VERSE (5)

THE CHURCH IS THE BUILDING TO PRAY AND SING.
IT'S WHERE MANY HAVE DISCOVERED THEIR THING.
THE CHOIR IS FULL WITH TALENTS OF CHEER,
IT MAKES YOU FEEL HAPPY JUST TO BE THERE.
SO FILL YOUR DAYS WITH JOY AND PEACE,
TO PURSUE THE DREAM WITH EXULTANT EASE.
THE GIVING OF THE OFFERING IS PLANTING THE SEED
TO HELP WITH THE ADVANCEMENT OF THE MINORITY'S CREED.

A BLESSED SONG

Action

DEC. 11, 2004

VERSE (1)

THE ACTION WILL SPEAK LOUDER THAN
THE WORD,
THIS IS NOT STRANGE, I AM SURE MANY
HAVE HEARD.
ITS WHAT IS DONE, SO DO IT RIGHT,
WHETHER THE PREFERENCE BE DAY OR
NIGHT.
ALLOW THE COURSE OF THOUGHT TO ACT
WITH PROPER DECISION;
WHICH WILL MAKE THINGS HAPPEN IN A
POSITIVE DIRECTION.

VERSE (2)

ACTION WILL REVEAL WHAT YOU REALLY
MEAN,
AND THE INTENDED PURPOSE WILL BE
SEEN.
CHOOSE THE SEQUENCE OF A PROJECT TO
BE THE TOOL,
AND THE RESULT OF THE ACT WILL BE
COOL.
BE CAREFUL AND USE THE SENSES
FOR GOOD BEHAVIOR HAS GOOD
CONSEQUENCES.

VERSE (3)

ACCOMPLISHMENT IS THE OUTCOME OF SOMETHING DONE,
WHICH CAN BE BRIGHT AS THE RAYS OF THE SUN.
SO MAKE THE EFFORT TO ACHIEVE THE GOAL
AND IT WILL BE FOREVER IMPRINTED IN THE SOUL.
THE DESIRE IS THE FULFILLMENT OF THE ACTION,
WHICH WILL PRODUCE BEYOND THE HIGHEST EXPECTATION.

A BLESSED SONG

A Pure Mind

DATE: OCT. 25, 2004

VERSE (1)

FILL YOUR MIND WITH A LOVELY THOUGHT, WHAT GOD HAS GIVEN YOU, CANNOT BE BOUGHT.
A PURE MIND IS ACKNOWLEDGED WITH HIGH ESTEEM
THE GIFT THAT SHOULD BE KEPT VERY CLEAN.
PUTTING YOUR CONSCIENCE TO THE TEST, THINKING ALONG THE LINES GOOD, BETTER, BEST.

VERSE (2)

A PURE MIND PORTRAYS POSITIVE ACTION,
USE IT RIGHT WITHOUT ANY CAUTION.
IT IS REMEDY FOR THE BODY AND MORE
WHEN ALL THINGS DO APPEAR PLEASANT
AND SURE.
A MIND SO RICH LIKE A DRINK OF WINE,
ONLY TIME CAN TELL WHAT YOU WILL
FIND.

VERSE (3)

OH! HOW WONDERFUL TO BE PURE IN MIND,
IT GIVES A SINCERE FEELING THAT JUST
SHOULD NOT BE LEFT BEHIND.
CLEAN THOUGHTS ARE LIKE THE WATER
FROM THE SPRING.
THAT ONLY NATURE ALONE CAN BRING

EULOGY –
Marcia Grace Stewart Goulbourne

Good morning, my name is Robert Whitely and I am a close friend of the family. Today, I have the honor of introducing you to Marcia Grace Goulbourne, and to reflect on her life and her legacy, as we say our final farewell to send her home with grace and dignity.

Marcia passes away on November 4th, 2018 at her residence after a long fight with cancer. Even though she was in tremendous pain, she never focused on her illness and never wanted to draw attention to it. While we know that she is now at peace and her struggles are at an end, there is still pain and sadness left behind and it would be her wish that everyone continue with their lives and be happy.

Marcia was born on May 5th, 1939, in Spanish Town, St Catherine, Jamaica. She was the second child of David and Icylyn Stewart, both deceased. She is sister to David Stewart, Jr. also deceased, and Peter Stewart whom you all know…and thank God he is here with us today.

Marcia's life was a simple one with good and honest intentions. She grew up in Spanish Town at 66 Young Street, the family home, amongst her brothers and cousins in what has been described as a disciplined household. She was considered the lady in the family. This is of no surprise as her father was a known police detective and the old Jamaican saying, "police pickney always bad," never applied to her. Coupled with that, was Grandma who was very loving and who kept a tight rein as well.

Marcia attended St. Catherine High School where she excelled in academics and sports, representing her school at the local level in Netball. After graduating high school, she worked at the Downtown Kingston Post Office. She then travelled to the USA, where she studied and became proficient in Data Processing.

Her stay in the US was brief, and she returned to Jamaica and pursued a new career path. She worked in Kingston for Bryden and Evelyn Ltd., The Jamaica Telephone Company and Sheraton Kingston Hotel as an Account Representative.

Marcia met and fell in love with her soul mate, Terrence Goulbourne while working at the Post Office. Marcia and Terrence got married in the 1960's and the union produced an only child, Donald.

One of the most important things in Marcia's life was music. She taught herself to play the piano and loved playing until she was no longer able. She particularly loved jazz and classical music, but enjoyed dancing to the beat of Rhythm and Blues. She often danced tirelessly at home with her older brother, David Jr., and could shake a leg at the popular dances held at the neighborhood Church Hall.

Growing up with her two brothers and cousins, Phyllis, Sissy, Stanley, and GraceAnn, was a most vibrant and memorable time for Marcia. Together they played and danced. They went to church together, fought together and got into mischief together. When one would do wrong, all would be scolded except Marcia. Being the lady, she would escape the punishment.

They were not city slickers; however, one could label them the Seven Brady Bunch. If you lived and went to school in Spanish Town, you knew of Detective D-Sam's Brady Bunch.

One of the most noticeable things about Marcia, is how she would light up when she recounted her childhood days. She enjoyed talking about the disciplined upbringing she had, and the times she spent with her brothers and cousins in Spanish Town.

In the early 1980s, with the hope of starting a new life, Marcia and Donald immigrated to the United States and settled in South Florida. Despite a spirited life in Jamaica, Marcia chose a new and quieter life here in America. She thrived in her own way of enjoying the quiet and solitude of life, and preferred spending time with her son and family.

She was a follower of Christ, spent time reading the scriptures and often remarked, "God Will Take Care Of It". She emphasized the importance of getting a good education to her son, and also passed on the love of music to him. She never waned in her support or love for him... Marcia and Donald were rarely apart.

He became her rock and her world. It was a bond that was solid and strong...and she was content with that. She always believed "family is the most important thing in life", a quality she inherited from her mother.

When her health began to fail, it was Donald who became her caretaker, and provided her with the opportunity to live out her years in a peaceful quiet manner.

Donald stepped up out of love, commitment, compassion and sense of duty, to honor the bond they shared. That's what families do! Of course, her brother Peter was always there for moral support.

Marcia is now reunited with her parents and her brother David, in a place that they prepared for her arrival.

Donald...may God bless you also. We know you'll certainly miss her, but she's finally home now in God's grace and care, and she's at peace...and smiling down at you.

Marcia...may the Angels go with you, and may God bless your soul.

In closing, I would like to share a special poem with you...but before I do, the family would like to take this opportunity to thank everyone for coming here today and sharing in this special moment.

2 TIMOTHY CHAPTER 4 VERSES 7 THROUGH 8

I have fought the good fight

I have finished the race

**Now there is in store for me the
crown of righteousness**

Which the Lord, the righteous Judge

Will award to me on that day – and not only to me

But also to all who have longed for his appearing.